SPORTSLINES

MEN'S & WOMEN'S GYMNASTICS

by
Jane Duden

CRESTWOOD HOUSE
New York

Maxwell Macmillan Canada
Toronto

Maxwell Macmillan International
New York Oxford Singapore Sydney

Library of Congress Cataloging-in-Publication Data
Duden, Jane
Men's & Women's Gymnastics / by Jane Duden.
p. cm. — (Sportslines)
Summary: Surveys the history, rules, and great moments of gymnastics.
ISBN 0-89686-727-7
1. Gymnastics—Juvenile literature. [1. Gymnastics.] I. Title. II Series.
GV461. D74 1992
796.44—dc20 91-24682

Photo Credits
Cover: AP—Wide World Photos (top), Dave Black (bottom)
The Bettmann Archive: 4, 7
AP—Wide World Photos: 9, 10, 13, 14, 16, 18, 20, 21, 22, 23, 24, 25
Dave Black: 26, 27, 29, 30, 31, 33, 34, 37, 38, 39, 40, 41, 42

CRESTWOOD HOUSE

Macmillan Publishing Company
866 Third Avenue
New York, NY 10022

Maxwell Macmillan Canada, Inc.
1200 Eglinton Avenue East
Suite 200
Don Mills, Ontario M3C 3N1

Macmillan Publishing Company is part of the Maxwell Communication Group of Companies.

Produced by Flying Fish Studio

Printed in the United States of America

First edition

10 9 8 7 6 5 4 3 2 1

Contents

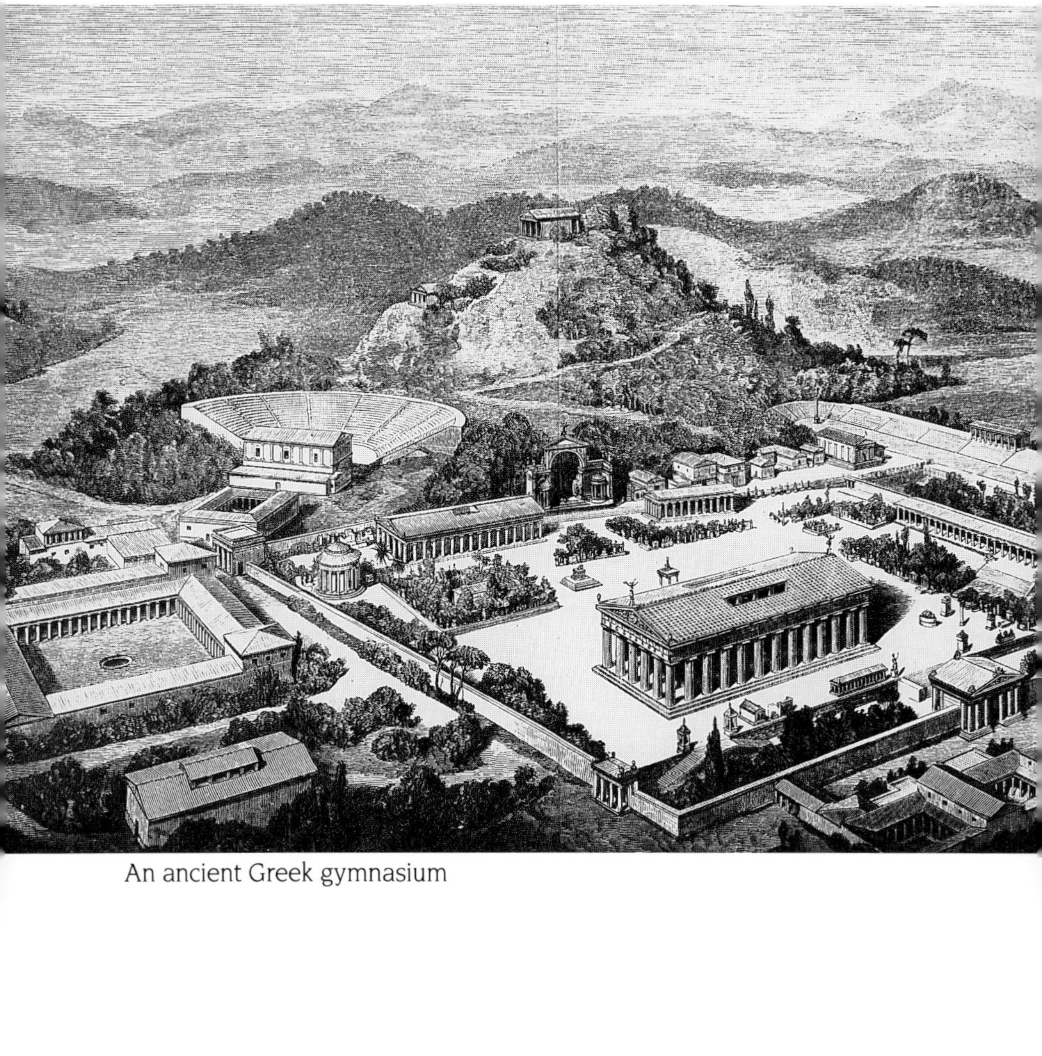

An ancient Greek gymnasium

Introduction

Gymnastics has been called the world's most beautiful sport. A lot of its popularity came from the television coverage of the last few Olympics. And a lot of it is from performers who become more thrilling each year. Sportslines *Gymnastics* shows and tells the story of gymnastics. Find out how it became one of the most popular Olympic sports today. Meet the greats, relive their historic feats, and get a peek at the future!

The Beginnings of Gymnastics

The words *gymnastics* and *gymnasium* came from the Greeks. The Greeks built the first gymnasiums about 2,500 years ago. Strong, healthy bodies were very important to them. Greek males spent a lot of time at the gyms. They all wanted to win events at the Olympics, the great sports competition of ancient Greece. The boys ran around the track, lifted weights, and climbed ropes. They threw the discus and the javelin. They jumped, tumbled, and wrestled.

Gymnastics, as we know it, was never part of the ancient Olympic Games. It was thought of as training for other sports. When the Romans conquered the Greeks, gymnastics was used for military training. The Romans added the wooden horse. But in A.D. 393, a Roman ruler cancelled the Olympic Games. The spread of Christianity led to less interest in the body and athletics. Many sports declined. For a long time gymnastics almost disappeared.

The Revival of Gymnastics

Gymnastics returned in the 1800s. Some men in Germany and Sweden started the comeback. They felt that gymnastics made children strong in mind and body, and should be part of school. One of these men was Friedrich Jahn, a German gymnastics coach. Many call him the father of gymnastics. Jahn invented the rings, the pommel horse, and the parallel bars. Peter Ling of Sweden also invented routines and apparatus. Ling invented free floor exercises, which evolved into the sport of rhythmic gymnastics. German and Swedish schools started gymnastics programs. Soon other countries followed their lead.

The International Gymnastics Federation (IFG)

As gymnastics spread, countries set up clubs. Clubs joined into groups called federations and associations. Germany had nearly 2,000 clubs by 1860. Poland, Holland, and France began federations. Belgium's federation invited other clubs to their festival in 1881. This meeting was the start of the world ties of gymnastics. People shared ideas. They set up rules and plans for competitions. They agreed to exclude professional gymnasts—those who competed for money. The group started as the European Gymnastics Federation. In 1921 that name became the Federation Internationale Gymnastique (FIG). In English, it's the International Gymnastics Federation (IFG).

Gymnastics and the Olympics

The revival of the Olympic Games gave a big boost to gymnastics. The first Olympics of the modern era was in

Athens, Greece, in 1896. Gymnastics was one of nine sports included. Seventy-five gymnasts from five countries competed. The equipment was similar to that used today. But the IFG didn't run the 1896 contests. Many of the world's best gymnasts did not compete. People just turned up and joined in. Contests were randomly added or left out. Gymnasts took part in events in which they had little or no experience. Teams brought their own apparatus. Sometimes it was rejected by organizers for not fitting the norm.

Crowds at the 1896 Olympic Games in Athens

Olympic Progress

In 1920 the IFG took over Olympic gymnastics. By 1924 in Paris, the Olympics gymnastics program was close to its present form. In 1928 women's gymnastics was added to the Olympics for the first time. Floor exercises were introduced at the 1932 Olympic Games in Los Angeles. For the first time, there were individual competitions in all apparatus events—parallel bars, floor exercises, horse vault, sidehorse, horizontal bar, and flying rings. Individual competitions were also held in tumbling, rope climbing, and club swinging. All were won by the United States. The Japanese participated for the first time in 1932. They made an astonishing showing.

Germany dominated the early Olympic Games. But the U.S. was making steady progress. In the 1956 Melbourne Games, only one American male had reached the top 30—John Beckner. No woman was in the leading 50. By Rome in 1960, three men were in the first 30. Three women had made the first 50.

Leaders Emerge

Soviet gymnasts made their first Olympic appearance at the Helsinki Games in 1952. They proved to be the best in the world. The Soviets won all of the individual events. They won the team titles for both men and women. The Soviets repeated this triumph at the 1956 Melbourne Games. But this time Japan was a close second to the Soviet Union.

At the 1960 Olympics in Rome, Japan took over. They took the team title from the Soviets for the first time. Japanese men began a 20-year reign over men's gymnastics. Americans were still in early stages in the sport, but better days were coming!

Soviet gymnast Larisa Latynina competing at the 1956 Games

The Tsukahara Vault

Mitsuo Tsukahara was a standout Japanese gymnast. At the Munich Olympics in 1972, he introduced his spectacular layout somersault (legs straight) with a full twist. He earned a 9.9 and won the vault. After Munich, everyone started using the "Tsukahara Vault." The popular stunt was called the "Sook" for short. The women adopted it, too. It showed a new level of daring acrobatics in women's gymnastics.

Soviet Superstars

At the 1976 Montreal Games, Nikolai Andrianov was the superstar. The Soviet gymnast won four gold, two silver, and one bronze medal. He won the individual all-around by a full point over Japan's closest rival, Sawao Kato.

The Swedish women's rhythmic gymnastics team

Rhythmic Gymnastics

In 1962 the IFG officially recognized modern rhythmic gymnastics. Artistic gymnastics showed off strength and tumbling ability. It was a youthful sport. But gymnasts were reaching their peaks at ever-younger ages. The IFG wanted a way to favor more mature gymnasts. Rhythmic gymnastics was the answer. The female-only sport was a test of grace and flexibility. Handsprings, walkovers, and aerials were not allowed. Instead, women used ropes, clubs, hoops, and balls in a mixture of body movements and dance. Ribbons were added in 1971.

The U.S. Gymnastics Federation

In 1963 the U.S. Gymnastics Federation (USGF) was formed. It governs the sport of gymnastics in the United States. The USGF is made up of 21 member associations. These 21 groups are the backbone of gymnastics in the U.S. They help athletes from grass roots to Olympic levels. A few of the 21 member groups are the Amateur Athletic Union, the American Turners, the National Collegiate Athletic Association, and the Young Men's Christian Association.

The USGF develops training programs and safety standards. It guides the growth and success of gymnastics in the United States. The USGF selects the U.S. national team for the Olympics. It assembles teams for the World Gymnastics Championships and the Pan-American Games. And it sends U.S. teams to many foreign nations each year for competitions and exhibitions.

The U.S. National Gymnastics Team

The ultimate honor for gymnasts is winning a place on the U.S. national gymnastics team. This is the team that competes at the Olympic Games. Each national team member works his or her way up through a series of qualifying meets. Each meet is a chance for the gymnast to advance. The men's team members usually come from colleges and universities. The women's team members most often come from private clubs and organizations.

Gymnasts who meet requirements can compete in the McDonald's U.S. Gymnastics Championships. The national team is chosen at these championships. A certain number of finishers in the men's and women's all-around events earn spots on the national team. The senior national team is for ages 15 and over. The junior national team for women is chosen from top finishers age 14 or younger. Twice a year, 30 boys age 10-18 are chosen for the junior national team for men.

Scoring

Gymnasts are scored on a scale of 1 to 10. Points are subtracted for faults in .1 of a point deductions. For example, falling off the apparatus is an automatic .5 penalty. Up to .2 of a point may be deducted for not landing with both feet touching the mat at the same time. Points may be deducted for failing to execute each compulsory exercise required for an apparatus. Compulsory exercises are identical stunts that everyone must do. The IFG says what they are. Compulsories are changed every four years. Gymnasts are also scored on optional exercises—original routines done by each gymnast.

Going for the Gold

The U.S. Gymnastic Team competes in several international meets. The most famous is the Olympics. The Olympic Games are held every four years. Other international meets are held every year. They are the World Championships, the Pan-American Games, and the World University Games.

A gymnastics meet is three events in one. Teams compete for a team championship. Individuals compete for the all-around championship. The individual apparatus championship is the third event.

Meet the Gymnasts:
Larisa Latynina—Crowd Pleaser

Larisa Latynina was a Soviet gymnast. Larisa helped establish the Soviet Union as the leader in women's team competition. She also set a trend of crowd pleasing that made women's gymnastics more well-known and popular.

Larisa's career shows how gymnastics has changed over the years. She won her first Olympic gold medal in 1956. She was already 22 years old. Then she won a gold medal in the world championship in 1958, while five months pregnant. She was back for the Olympics in Rome in 1960. Larisa won a record 18 Olympic medals, nine of them gold. In 1964 she won her last Olympic gold on floor exercises in Tokyo. She was almost 30 years old!

Larisa Latynina

Larisa belonged to a different era of gymnasts. It was an era of adult women. They impressed judges with precision, grace, and character. Today's gymnastic stars are younger. They are usually in their teens. They impress with daring, pizazz, and energy.

Queen of the 1968 Mexico City Games

Television was bringing gymnastics into world view. In 1964 and 1968, the world watched Vera Caslavska become a champion. Vera was from Czechoslovakia. At the Olympics in 1968, she added four gold medals to the three she had won in Tokyo in 1964. Vera added more romance and drama by getting married during the Games. Then she retired. Vera was also the first gymnast to put sparkle into her performance. She charmed audiences with every move. Vera paved the way for a young Russian gymnast to change traditional gymnastics forever.

Vera Caslavska

Here Comes Olga!

In 1972 the Soviet Gymnastic Federation gave their "Master of Sport" award to a talented 16-year-old. Her name was Olga Korbut. Olga did a new trick on uneven bars in competition. She did a layout back off the high bar and then regrasped the high bar. Olga then went on to perform a back somersault ("somi") on every event. She was the first woman gymnast ever to accomplish that feat.

Olga was the first gymnast to perform daring stunts on the beam. Thus, she realized the need for added comfort and safety. Olga asked that padding be placed on and under the balance beam. She got her request. Today, thanks to Olga, thick padding mounted on springs is placed under every apparatus.

Olga brought her daring stunts and bubbly personality to the Olympics in 1972. She not only won medals and fame. She did something no other gymnast had ever done before—she paid attention to the audience. She smiled and waved at them. And she won their hearts. Olga Korbut set gymnastics aflame with a new style.

No More Blunders

The all-around competition at the 1972 Olympic Games was nearly over. Olga Korbut seemed to have the most coveted Olympic title in her grasp. Then she stubbed her toe during a performance on the uneven bars. Olga struggled through the rest of her routine. But her concentration was broken. When she saw her low score, she burst into tears. She finished a disappointing seventh all-around. A worldwide

Olga Korbut's tragedy on the uneven bars

television audience watched. They wept with her. The crowd booed the judges. "Little Olga," the 4-foot 11-inch, 85-pound Soviet, was their favorite.

Olga told reporters, "I will not make any more blunders." And she didn't. The next day she won gold medals in balance beam and floor exercises. She also won a silver medal on the bars. Olga was the darling of the 1972 Olympics. "Olga" became a household name. She brought gymnastics new fame.

Nancy Thies's New Trick

Fifteen-year-old Nancy Thies was on the U.S. women's team that went to Munich in 1972. She had trained long and hard to perfect a new move. Aerial work (tumbling without hands touching the beam) had never been done in the Olympics. Nancy changed that! She did an aerial back somersault, earning rip-roaring cheers! It was the first aerial back somersault ever performed in the Olympic Games.

Several hours later, Olga Korbut also performed an aerial back somersault on the balance beam. The world had followed Olga's every move during the Munich Games. Olga was given the credit as first person to perform that move on the balance beam in the Olympic Games. It was a disappointment for Nancy. Still, when all the scores were tallied, there was something to celebrate. The U.S. women's team finished fourth. It was the highest ranking ever received by an American women's gymnastic team!

A year later, Nancy Thies won the National Balance Beam Championship. A sportswriter described her routine: "She completed a back somersault. It was fluid—almost as if it had not been less than a year since Russia's Olga Korbut laid it on the judges for the first time last September in Munich."

America Discovers Women's Gymnastics

When America discovered Olga Korbut, America discovered women's gymnastics. Olga's elfin charm won the hearts of a worldwide television audience. Suddenly parents started taking their daughters to gymnastic classes. They dreamed of creating the next Olga. American superstars were on their way!

Crowd favorite Nadia Comaneci

Nadia

The 1976 Olympic Games in Montreal brought the next superstar. Nadia Comaneci was a 14-year-old from Romania. Nadia had been trained as a gymnast since the age of six. Her coach was Bela Karolyi. Nadia was already well-known to experts. In 1975 she was European all-around gymnastics champion. She had toppled the five-time European champion Lyudmila Tourischeva of the Soviet Union.

At Montreal, Nadia captured the worldwide TV audience. This serious, quiet young gymnast did even more daring stunts than Olga. And during the team competition, she made Olympic history. Nadia scored a 10—a perfect score. No one had ever earned 10 at the Olympics before! The scoreboards could only go as high as 9.99. Then they were fixed to show 10. Then Nadia scored 10 six more times! Four were for her work on the uneven bars. Three were for performances on the balance beam. Nadia won the all-around championship. She also won two golds for her work on the balance beam and uneven bars.

Sue Soffe's Gold

Sue Soffe was the first American to take home the gold in an international contest for rhythmic gymnastics. She won a gold medal at the 1978 Pan-Pacific International Championships. Sue had turned to rhythmic gymnastics in the early 1970s. Artistic gymnastics had been her life. But the hard landings had badly hurt Sue's ankles. She had to choose between gymnastics or the ability to walk later in life. Sue slowly turned her attention to rhythmic gymnastics. Her efforts paid off with a gold medal.

The U.S. Olympic Festival: Training for Olympians

In 1978 the U.S. Olympic Festival began under the name of the National Sports Festival. It provided America's Olympic hopefuls a chance to compete in an Olympic-style event. It is held every non-Olympic summer in cities across the country. It became the U.S. Olympic Festival in 1986. The change helped the public identify the festival's role in the Olympic movement.

The 1979 Olympic Festival was held in Colorado Springs, Colorado. This is the headquarters of the United States Olympic Committee. In men's gymnastics, Bart Conner was tops. He took four gold medals, three silvers, and one bronze. Conner was a member of the 1976, 1980, and 1984 Olympic teams. He went on to stardom at the Los Angeles Games. For the women, 1980 and 1984 Olympian Tracee Talavera won three golds, including the all-around title.

The 1981 Olympic Festival was in Syracuse, New York. Ron Galimore scored a perfect 10 in the men's vault event. It was the first perfect score by a male gymnast in festival history. Mark Caso won the gold medal for his work on the still rings. Mark won five total medals less than two years after a broken neck had nearly ended his life. In women's competition, a little-known Mary Lou Retton was the all-around silver medalist.

Bart Conner

Kurt Thomas

The American Flag Goes Up!

The 1979 World Championships was a huge success for American gymnasts. The Japanese and the Soviet men were still dominant. But they had to be at their best to match the American men. Kurt Thomas and Bart Conner shone. Between them, they won three gold medals, three silver, and a bronze in individual events. Thomas said: "For so long, our flag has been down in the box somewhere during the medal ceremonies. Now it was up there almost every time. It was a great feeling."

Nadia goes for the gold on the beam.

Nadia's Last Olympic Medals

Nadia was back at the 1980 Olympic Games in Moscow. Would she win the contest for all-around champion? She needed 9.95 to win. A 9.9 would mean she'd share the gold medal. The arena watched in total silence as Nadia performed. It seemed as if she had made it. But for 28 minutes the judges argued over her score. Nadia lost the all-around gold medal when judges from Poland and the Soviet Union gave her 9.85 on her balance beam performance. It was just low enough to give Russian gymnast Yelena Davydova the title. The next day Nadia took first place in the beam and the floor exercises. She won an Olympic total of five gold medals, three silver, and one bronze.

Nadia planned to enter the 1984 Olympics. However, six weeks before the Los Angeles Games, a Romanian official made a puzzling announcement. Nadia would not be coming to the 1984 Olympics as a gymnastic team member. She had retired from competition. Nadia was 22 years old.

A Medal for Every Category

Alexander Ditiatin, Soviet gymnast, earned the spotlight at the 1980 Olympics in Moscow. He scored the first perfect 10 in men's Olympic competition. The powerful Ditiatin became the first person to win eight medals in a single Olympics. He is the only male gymnast to win Olympic medals in all eight categories!

Alexander Ditiatin

The Americans Lose a Turn

American athletes did not compete at the 1980 Olympics. The United States called for a boycott because the Games were in Moscow. The boycott was in response to the Soviets' refusal to move their troops out of Afghanistan. Japan and many other countries joined the United States in the boycott. Without Japan's gymnasts to beat, the Soviets had an easy time winning their first team title in 24 years.

A Famous Coach

Bela Karolyi was Nadia's first coach. He was behind Romania's rise as a world gymnastics power. He believed in an open spirit and search for excellence. That quality brought him coaching triumphs. It also brought him troubles, mostly with the Romanian government. In 1981 the Romanian team was touring the United States. On the last day, Mr. and Mrs. Karolyi chose not to show up for the flight home. They stayed in the United States to make a new life. Within a year, they had opened their own gym in Houston, Texas. Soon Karolyi drew America's top gymnasts to his school.

Bela Karolyi and his family become American citizens.

Mary Lou Retton

Mary Lou and the McDonald's Cup Meet

In March 1983 Mary Lou Retton made her debut in international gymnastics. She had enrolled at Karolyi's school. One of her teammates on the U.S. women's Olympic gymnastic team had been injured. That's when Mary Lou went as an alternate to the McDonald's American Cup Meet. This meet is the most prestigious of the international gymnastics meets held in the United States. By the end of the meet, Mary Lou Retton had won the individual events championship on the vault and floor exercises. She tied for first place on the uneven bars. And she won the women's all-around gold medal! Mary Lou had topped the Soviet Union's all-around champion and Bulgaria's world vault champion.

A year later at the 1984 McDonald's Cup Meet, Mary Lou gave a repeat performance. She scored a 39.50 out of a possible 40. She won the women's all-around gold for the second year in a row. Her next stop was the 1984 Olympics! The world was about to meet Mary Lou.

Kathy Johnson

A Dream Come True

Kathy Johnson won a bronze on the balance beam at the Olympics in 1984. At 24, she was known as the "old lady" of gymnastics. Kathy had a shining eight-year career on the U.S. national team. Eight years is average for many sports, but unusual in gymnastics—a sport for youngsters. Her goal was to win an Olympic medal. Kathy had many ups and downs in her long career. A broken foot bone once kept her away from gymnastics for eight months. The U.S. boycott of the Moscow Games took away her chance to try in 1980. But she qualified for more major U.S. national teams (Olympic and World Championship) than any gymnast in the history of the sport. In 1984 her Olympic dream came true. Then Kathy retired. In all, she won two Olympic and two World Championship medals. She won eight National Championships.

Soviet Boycott Opens the Door

The Soviet women's team had won eight consecutive Olympic titles. They would have been favored to win again in Los Angeles. But the Soviet government stopped them from competing in 1984. The Soviet boycott opened the door for other hopeful gymnasts to shine. And they did! The 1984 Olympic Games in Los Angeles was America's year.

Rhythmic Gymnastics Goes to the Olympics

The sport of rhythmic gymnastics made its official debut at the Olympics in 1984. In this female-only sport, women use ribbons, ropes, clubs, hoops, and balls in a mixture of body movements and dance. They are accompanied by music, which can come from only one instrument—usually a piano. They perform in 60-90 second routines on a 1,550-feet- (12-meter-) square floor mat. The trick is to keep the apparatus moving at all times. The routine must flow continuously. Performers juggle, throw, and twirl as they compete to win.

A display of rhythmic gymnastics

The first Olympics for rhythmic gymnastics got off to a sad start. The world's top rhythmic gymnasts were absent. Bulgaria and the Soviet Union had taken all the top spots at the previous world championships. But the Soviet boycott kept them away. Still, a beautiful new sport had won a deserving place on the Olympic program.

America's Shining Star

Ever since Olga Korbut melted hearts in 1972, U.S. sports fans wondered when America would have a female gymnastics star. It happened in 1984 at the Los Angeles Olympic Games. She was a piston-driven pixie named Mary Lou Retton. Her coach was Bela Karolyi.

It wasn't until Mary Lou Retton won at the 1984 Olympics that everybody knew about her. No American woman gymnast had ever won an Olympic gold medal. But now Mary Lou Retton was close. She had to score a perfect 10 on her vault to win the gold medal in the all-around. Any less and she would tie Ecaterina Szabo for first place. Mary Lou did not want to tie. She wanted to win. At the signal, Mary Lou exploded down the runway. The move was a layout back somersault with a double twist. She performed it flawlessly and nailed a perfect 10. Even before her score was up, Mary Lou knew the gold belonged to her. "I knew by my takeoff that I had it. I knew by my vault that I had it. I knew it when I was in the air!" Everyone else in the audience knew it, too. Yet she still had to take her second vault. The rules say the best of two. Even though she couldn't score any higher, Mary Lou knew what an Olympic champion would do. She went to the vault

Mary Lou celebrates her perfect scores.

runway and scored a 10 all over again! The 16-year-old Retton had won the all-around title, marking her as the best woman gymnast in the world. It was a first for the United States. Mary Lou Retton ended up with one gold medal, two silvers, two bronzes, and instant fame!

The U.S. Men's Team

China was expected to prevail in men's gymnastics at the Los Angeles Olympics. They were the reigning world champions. But the Americans had a surprise in store. The U.S. team of six included Peter Vidmar, Mitch Gaylord, Tim Daggett, Bart Conner, Scott Johnson, and James Hartung. They scored high enough points to win America's first gold medal for team competition in Olympic history!

• Peter Vidmar's perfect 10 score on the side horse helped the U.S. take the lead midway through the team competition.

• Tim Daggett's perfect 10 on the horizontal bar during the team event clinched the U.S. team victory. Tim also won a bronze medal for the pommel horse, his favorite apparatus.

Peter Vidmar

Mitch Gaylord

• Mitch is perhaps most well-known for his original stunt, the "Gaylord II." Mitch does a flyaway backflip with a half-twist, then recatches the bar in an undergrip, all in a blink of an eye.

• Bart Conner at 26 was the oldest team member. The parallel bars were Bart's specialty. He won the gold medal in the individual events at the 1984 Olympics.

After the 1984 Olympics, when the U.S. men gymnasts won the team championship, even their coach said, "No one who knows gymnastics thought we'd beat the Chinese. I never thought I'd see this in my lifetime."

Gymnastics Fever

The 1984 Olympics in Los Angeles gave America gymnastics fever. Soaring numbers of young people wanted to take gymnastics lessons. They dreamed of going for the gold on balance beams, parallel bars, and vaulting horses. Less than two months after the 1984 Olympics, Bela Karolyi signed up 600 new students. That was twice the normal size of his gymnastic school in Houston, Texas.

The "New Gymnasts" and the "Wow" Factor

With her raw nerve and mental and physical strength, Mary Lou Retton was typical of the "new gymnasts." At 4 feet, 9 inches tall, she was a pint-sized pack of power and determination.

The new gymnasts have turned "ballet gymnastics" into "power gymnastics." They focus on original and thrilling acrobatic stunts. These stunts take great strength and concentration. They work to create a "wow" factor in their routines. Judges call this wow factor "ROV." ROV stands for risk, originality, and virtuosity. Mitch Gaylord sums it up: "Today's gymnasts go for the big trick, the 'killer move' that leaves judges and spectators staring wide-eyed and openmouthed."

Brandy

In 1981 little Brandy Johnson's doctor suggested that tumbling classes would help her recover from surgery. He warned her parents not to be disappointed if she could barely do a sit-up. But Brandy surprised them all. She decided she wanted to be a world-known gymnast and compete in the

Brandy Johnson

1988 Olympics. She started by moving with her family from Tallahassee to Altamonte Springs, Florida, to train with Coach Kevin Brown. Nine months before the 1988 Olympics, Brandy moved again to Houston, Texas, to train with Bela Karolyi. Some said she was too young to make the Olympic team. But Brandy made the Olympic squad that traveled to Seoul, South Korea. And she became the highest placing U.S. gymnast! Brandy finished tenth overall and fifth in the vault. She had planned on quitting gymnastics after the Olympics. But the thrill of success led her on.

1989 U.S. National Gymnastics Championships

Brandy Johnson and Tim Ryan were the top winners at the U.S. National Gymnastics Championships. The events were held in July at the Met Center in Bloomington, Minnesota. This was the most important competition in the United States. World Championship competition came next for those who qualified.

As Brandy's floor music at the 1989 U.S. Championships proclaimed, she was "Hot Stuff." Brandy won three out of four event titles. She became the vault, beam, and floor champion. She outscored her nearest competitor by nearly two points!

Tim Ryan

Tim Ryan won the U.S. men's title. Tim was 18. He became the youngest national men's champion since former U.S. Olympian Bart Conner. Bart was 17 years old when he won in 1975. Tim had come up from 23rd place in the 1988 U.S. Championships. Second place went to Lance Ringnald. Third all-around went to Mike Racanelli. The top 12 gymnasts made up the U.S. Senior National Team.

Training for World Championships

World Championship competition is held every two years. The United States won no medals in the finals of the 1987 World Championships. The U.S. men placed ninth. The women placed sixth. They hoped to change that in 1989! The World Championships were held October 1989 in Stuttgart, Germany. It was the 25th year for the World Championships competition.

Indianapolis, Indiana is the site of the USGF National Gymnastics Center. The men's and women's senior teams train there for the World Championships. Team members compete against each other. The top seven traveled to Stuttgart for the 1989 world competition. The 1989 Olympic Festival had given them a chance to practice together before the World Championships.

A Good Year at the World Championships

In 1989 Brandy Johnson was one of the strongest U.S. gymnasts going to the World Championships. At the 1989 World Championships she led the U.S. to its highest finish ever (fourth). She tied for the highest all-around finish ever (seventh). And she won a silver medal in the vault.

She's Got Rhythm

Caroline Hunt was one of the best rhythmic gymnasts in the United States. In 1990 she began competing in the junior division, which is for top gymnasts ages 12 to 14. She had won every state, regional, and national junior event she entered. Caroline won the junior division at the 1990 Rhythmic National Championships in Eugene, Oregon. She scored 36.85 points out of a possible 40. It was higher than the score of any other junior *or* senior gymnast! (The senior division is for top gymnasts age 14 and older.) Caroline hopes to compete at the 1996 Summer Olympics when she will be 18 years old.

1990 Olympic Festival

The 1990 Olympic Festival was very important to the rhythmic gymnasts. They were competing for a spot on the World Championship team. Three gymnasts and an alternate would go to the World Championships in Sarajevo, Yugoslavia in September.

Diane Simpson won the all-around title in rhythmic gymnastics at the 1990 Olympic Festival in Oklahoma. Alexandra Feldman and Jenifer Lovell also earned the right to compete at the World Championships.

It was the third Olympic Festival title for Simpson. She won the event in 1986 and 1989. Diane had finished 26th in the 1988 Olympics in Seoul. Diane Simpson is credited with helping make rhythmic gymnastics more popular in the United States.

Diane switched from artistic gymnastics and figure skating to rhythmic gymnastics at the age of 12. Now Diane is 21, a

Diane Simpson

junior at Northwestern University. And even though she may be the school's best athlete, Diane is rarely recognized on campus. Diane said: "Rhythmic gymnastics was so new in the U.S. that when I started, no one really knew what it was. Most people don't know much about it, but I think that's changing."

Kim Zmeskal: Up-and-Comer

She was only 14 years old, but Kim Zmeskal was the top American female gymnast for 1990. Kim is from Houston, Texas. She trains at Karolyi's Gymnastics. Despite the fact that she's so young, Kim has a long list of accomplishments. She was the 1990 U.S. Nationals Champion. Kim won the all-around titles at the 1990 U.S. Gymnastics Championships, the McDonald's American Cup, and the U.S. Challenge. The McDonald's American Cup draws world-class gymnasts from the United States, the Soviet Union, Germany, Romania, Japan, and other countries.

Kim Zmeskal and coach Bela Karolyi

Kim scored four perfect 10s in 1990. One came at a meet in Switzerland. Next she scored 10s on vault and floor exercise at the 1990 Challenge in Las Vegas, Nevada. In August, Kim scored a 10 on the vault at a major meet between the United States and the Soviet Union. The meet was the McDonald's Challenge: USA-USSR in San Jose, California.

Kim's national teammates voted her "1990 Athlete of the Year." The Women's Sports Foundation gave Kim the "1990 Up-and-Comer" award in the artistic category. The award honors ten female athletes who show the promise of becoming America's next world champions. All this...after only eight years in gymnastics!

The Goodwill Games

The Goodwill Games were held in Tacoma/Spokane, Washington, in July 1990. The world's best athletes in 21 sports were invited. The Goodwill Games promote friendship and understanding among athletes and countries around the world. They give athletes from many sports a chance to compete in a worldwide event between Summer Olympics. The 1990 Goodwill Games fell between the Seoul Olympics of 1988 and the Barcelona Olympics in 1992. They brought two rising American gymnasts closer to the top: Betty Okino and Chris Waller.

The U.S. Men's Team at the 1990 Goodwill Games

Betty Okino Makes Her Move

Only a short time ago, Betty Okino was an unknown newcomer. In 1989 Betty did not qualify for the Junior National team. Then in 1990, 15-year-old Betty skipped the junior division and placed second all-around in the senior division at the U.S. Championships. That made her the No. 2 ranked gymnast in the United States in 1990! Betty earned a spot on the 1990 Goodwill Games team. She was the top finisher for the United States at the Goodwill Games and placed fourth in the all-around overall. Betty's performance there was the best by an American. Betty also helped the United States team earn the silver medal.

Betty Okino

Chris Waller

Chris Waller: No. 2

Chris Waller of UCLA finished 12th at the 1989 U.S. Championships. He barely made the U.S. national team. But at the 1990 Goodwill Games, Chris became the No. 2 ranked men's gymnast in the United States. He helped the U.S. men gain a stunning second place finish—their biggest finish since the 1984 Olympic Games. Chris credits a new attitude for his rise to the top. Instead of worrying about missing, he tells himself he can do it. Then he does it! The 1991 World Championships are Chris's next goal.

The 1990 World Cup

The eighth World Cup gymnastics competition for men and women was held in Belgium in October 1990. The top 19 women and 20 men from 14 countries vied for the all-around title. Brandy Johnson, Sandy Woolsey, and Lance Ringnald represented the United States. Lance finished 15th. Brandy finished fifth, showing she was on the comeback trail.

In 1990 illness and injury gave Brandy a dismal start. She finished 22nd at the 1990 McDonald's American Cup. But she stormed back. Brandy finished third at the 1990 U.S. Gymnastics Championships. She won the vault and floor titles. She breezed through the 1990 Olympic Festival in a class by herself, setting records on the way. And by the 1990 World Cup, Brandy was back in top form. Her fifth place finish was the highest ever achieved by a U.S. gymnast at the World Cup.

Queen Yankee

Shannon Miller was a 13-year-old, 66-pound dynamo when she went to the Women's Tournament in Catania, Italy in 1990. She was such a hit that people there called her Queen Yankee. Shannon won the all-around competition and three individual event finals.

Shannon Miller

Brandy Bids Good-Bye

Fans were hoping to watch Brandy Johnson win an Olympic medal at Barcelona in 1992. But Brandy had her sights set on a college degree instead. In 1991 she traded in her handgrips and leotards for schoolbooks. Due to injuries and burnout, Brandy was retiring. She said: "I've made my goals. The 1992 Olympics were never a goal—they were an option. I've had my time, now the other girls can shine."

With the growth of gymnastics in the United States, there will be plenty of new stars to shine!

Gymnastics Timelines

1903: The first World Championships were held in Antwerp, Belgium, August 14-18. France, Belgium, Luxembourg, and Holland took part.

1931: The first national Women's Gymnastic Championship was won by Roberta C. Ranck of Philadelphia. The contest was held in Springfield, Massachusetts.

1932: Floor exercises were first held as an individual Olympic event.

1940: The first intercollegiate gymnastics team championship was held. The University of Illinois in Chicago won even though three clubs had more points. The others had only one member each, so were not eligible for the team championship.

1949: The IFG ruled that organizers of championships had to provide their own equipment.

1952: Women first competed in individual events in the Olympics.

1952: The Russian men gymnasts won the team title at the World Gymnastics Championships. Until 1983 they took the team title every year except for 1960 and 1964 when the Japanese won.

1960: Japan's Masao Takemoto became the oldest gymnast in Olympic history to win a gold medal. He was 40.

1961: Gymnasts from the Soviet Union came to America. Their visit started a tradition that has continued regularly ever since. Their first American tour included a men's competition at Penn State University.

1970: At the World Gymnastics Championships, Cathy Rigby became the first American gymnast, male or female, to win a medal. She earned a silver on the balance beam.

1976: The American Cup was founded as a special international event to celebrate the U.S. Bicentennial. It has been held every year. Nadia Comaneci, unknown outside her country, won the first American Cup. A few months later she made gymnastics history at the Montreal Olympics by scoring seven 10s.

1978: The U.S. Olympic Festival began under the name of the National Sports Festival.

1983: The Chinese men's gymnastic team won the 1983 World Championships, beating the number one ranked Soviet Union.

1983: Mary Lou Retton became the first American woman to win Japan's Chunichi Cup.

1984: Mary Lou Retton was named sportswoman of the year by *Sports Illustrated* magazine.

1985: Mary Lou Retton became the first woman gymnast to win three McDonald's American Cup all-around championships. In 1985 she became the first gymnast to be elected to the U.S. Olympic Hall of Fame.

1986: Scott Johnson increased his all-time Olympic Festival medal total to 22. He won one medal in each of his sport's eight events. Scott tied the 1979 Festival record set by his Olympic teammate Bart Conner.

1988: Olga Korbut was the first gymnast to be inducted into the International Gymnastics Hall of Fame, located in Oceanside, California.

1991: For the first time in 12 years the World Gymnastics Championships were held in the United States. The top men's and women's gymnastics teams from around the world competed in Indianapolis, Indiana, September 6-15, to determine who would compete in the 1992 Summer Olympics.

Index